GIFT LOG

Gift Log

Party For

Date	Gift Received	Given By	Thank You?

Gift Log

Party For

Date	Gift Received	Given By	Thank You?

Gift Log

Party For

Date	Gift Received	Given By	Thank You?

Gift Log

Party For

Date	Gift Received	Given By	Thank You?

Gift Log

Party For

Date	Gift Received	Given By	Thank You?

Gift Log

Party For

Date	Gift Received	Given By	Thank You?

Gift Log

Party For

Date	Gift Received	Given By	Thank You?

Gift Log

Party For

Date	Gift Received	Given By	Thank You?

Gift Log

Party For

Date	Gift Received	Given By	Thank You?

Gift Log

Party For

Date	Gift Received	Given By	Thank You?

Gift Log

Party For

Date	Gift Received	Given By	Thank You?

Gift Log

Party For

Date	Gift Received	Given By	Thank You?

Gift Log

Party For

Date	Gift Received	Given By	Thank You?

Gift Log

Party For

Date	Gift Received	Given By	Thank You?

Gift Log

Party For

Date	Gift Received	Given By	Thank You?

Gift Log

Party For

Date	Gift Received	Given By	Thank You?

Gift Log

Party For

Date	Gift Received	Given By	Thank You?

Gift Log

Party For

Date	Gift Received	Given By	Thank You?

Gift Log

Party For

Date	Gift Received	Given By	Thank You?

Gift Log

Party For

Date	Gift Received	Given By	Thank You?

Gift Log

Party For

Date	Gift Received	Given By	Thank You?

Gift Log

Party For

Date	Gift Received	Given By	Thank You?

Gift Log

Party For

Date	Gift Received	Given By	Thank You?

Gift Log

Party For

Date	Gift Received	Given By	Thank You?

Gift Log

Party For

Date	Gift Received	Given By	Thank You?

Gift Log

Party For

Date	Gift Received	Given By	Thank You?

Gift Log

Party For

Date	Gift Received	Given By	Thank You?

Gift Log

Party For

Date	Gift Received	Given By	Thank You?

Gift Log

Party For

Date	Gift Received	Given By	Thank You?

Gift Log

Party For

Date	Gift Received	Given By	Thank You?

Gift Log

Party For

Date	Gift Received	Given By	Thank You?

Gift Log

Party For

Date	Gift Received	Given By	Thank You?

Gift Log

Party For

Date	Gift Received	Given By	Thank You?

Gift Log

Party For

Date	Gift Received	Given By	Thank You?

Gift Log

Party For

Date	Gift Received	Given By	Thank You?

Gift Log

Party For

Date	Gift Received	Given By	Thank You?

Gift Log

Party For

Date	Gift Received	Given By	Thank You?

Gift Log

Party For

Date	Gift Received	Given By	Thank You?

Gift Log

Party For

Date	Gift Received	Given By	Thank You?

Gift Log

Party For

Date	Gift Received	Given By	Thank You?

Gift Log

Party For

Date	Gift Received	Given By	Thank You?

Gift Log

Party For

Date	Gift Received	Given By	Thank You?

Gift Log

Party For

Date	Gift Received	Given By	Thank You?

Gift Log

Party For

Date	Gift Received	Given By	Thank You?

Gift Log

Party For

Date	Gift Received	Given By	Thank You?

Gift Log

Party For

Date	Gift Received	Given By	Thank You?

Gift Log

Party For

Date	Gift Received	Given By	Thank You?

Gift Log

Party For

Date	Gift Received	Given By	Thank You?

Gift Log

Party For

Date	Gift Received	Given By	Thank You?

Gift Log

Party For

Date	Gift Received	Given By	Thank You?

Gift Log

Party For

Date	Gift Received	Given By	Thank You?

Gift Log

Party For

Date	Gift Received	Given By	Thank You?

Gift Log

Party For

Date	Gift Received	Given By	Thank You?

Gift Log

Party For

Date	Gift Received	Given By	Thank You?

Gift Log

Party For

Date	Gift Received	Given By	Thank You?

Gift Log

Party For

Date	Gift Received	Given By	Thank You?

Gift Log

Party For

Date	Gift Received	Given By	Thank You?

Gift Log

Party For

Date	Gift Received	Given By	Thank You?

Gift Log

Party For

Date	Gift Received	Given By	Thank You?

Gift Log

Party For

Date	Gift Received	Given By	Thank You?

Gift Log

Party For

Date	Gift Received	Given By	Thank You?

Gift Log

Party For

Date	Gift Received	Given By	Thank You?

Gift Log

Party For

Date	Gift Received	Given By	Thank You?

Gift Log

Party For

Date	Gift Received	Given By	Thank You?

Gift Log

Party For

Date	Gift Received	Given By	Thank You?

Gift Log

Party For

Date	Gift Received	Given By	Thank You?

Gift Log

Party For

Date	Gift Received	Given By	Thank You?

Gift Log

Party For

Date	Gift Received	Given By	Thank You?

Gift Log

Party For

Date	Gift Received	Given By	Thank You?

Gift Log

Party For

Date	Gift Received	Given By	Thank You?

Gift Log

Party For

Date	Gift Received	Given By	Thank You?

Gift Log

Party For

Date	Gift Received	Given By	Thank You?

Gift Log

Party For

Date	Gift Received	Given By	Thank You?

Gift Log

Party For

Date	Gift Received	Given By	Thank You?

Gift Log

Party For

Date	Gift Received	Given By	Thank You?

Gift Log

Party For

Date	Gift Received	Given By	Thank You?

Gift Log

Party For

Date	Gift Received	Given By	Thank You?

Gift Log

Party For

Date	Gift Received	Given By	Thank You?

Gift Log

Party For

Date	Gift Received	Given By	Thank You?

Gift Log

Party For

Date	Gift Received	Given By	Thank You?

Gift Log

Party For

Date	Gift Received	Given By	Thank You?

Gift Log

Party For

Date	Gift Received	Given By	Thank You?

Gift Log

Party For

Date	Gift Received	Given By	Thank You?

Gift Log

Party For

Date	Gift Received	Given By	Thank You?

Gift Log

Party For

Date	Gift Received	Given By	Thank You?

Gift Log

Party For

Date	Gift Received	Given By	Thank You?

Gift Log

Party For

Date	Gift Received	Given By	Thank You?

Gift Log

Party For

Date	Gift Received	Given By	Thank You?

Gift Log

Party For

Date	Gift Received	Given By	Thank You?

Gift Log

Party For

Date	Gift Received	Given By	Thank You?

Gift Log

Party For

Date	Gift Received	Given By	Thank You?

Gift Log

Party For

Date	Gift Received	Given By	Thank You?

Gift Log

Party For

Date	Gift Received	Given By	Thank You?

Gift Log

Party For

Date	Gift Received	Given By	Thank You?

Gift Log

Party For

Date	Gift Received	Given By	Thank You?

Gift Log

Party For

Date	Gift Received	Given By	Thank You?

Gift Log

Party For

Date	Gift Received	Given By	Thank You?

Gift Log

Party For

Date	Gift Received	Given By	Thank You?

Gift Log

Party For

Date	Gift Received	Given By	Thank You?

Gift Log

Party For

Date	Gift Received	Given By	Thank You?

Gift Log

Party For

Date	Gift Received	Given By	Thank You?

Gift Log

Party For

Date	Gift Received	Given By	Thank You?

Gift Log

Party For

Date	Gift Received	Given By	Thank You?

Gift Log

Party For

Date	Gift Received	Given By	Thank You?

Gift Log

Party For

Date	Gift Received	Given By	Thank You?

Gift Log

Party For

Date	Gift Received	Given By	Thank You?

Gift Log

Party For

Date	Gift Received	Given By	Thank You?

Gift Log

Party For

Date	Gift Received	Given By	Thank You?

Gift Log

Party For

Date	Gift Received	Given By	Thank You?

Gift Log

Party For

Date	Gift Received	Given By	Thank You?

Gift Log

Party For

Date	Gift Received	Given By	Thank You?

Gift Log

Party For

Date	Gift Received	Given By	Thank You?

Gift Log

Party For

Date	Gift Received	Given By	Thank You?

Gift Log

Party For

Date	Gift Received	Given By	Thank You?

Gift Log

Party For

Date	Gift Received	Given By	Thank You?

Gift Log

Party For

Date	Gift Received	Given By	Thank You?

Gift Log

Party For

Date	Gift Received	Given By	Thank You?

Gift Log

Party For

Date	Gift Received	Given By	Thank You?

Gift Log

Party For

Date	Gift Received	Given By	Thank You?

www.ingramcontent.com/pod-product-compliance
Lightning Source LLC
Chambersburg PA
CBHW050743030426
42336CB00012B/1626